Yoga
For Weight
Loss

Monique Joiner Siedlak

OSHUN
PUBLICATIONS

Printed in the United States of America

Second Edition 2018

ISBN-13: 978-1-948834-56-8

Publisher
www.oshunpublications.com

Disclaimer
All the material contained in this book is provided for educational and informational purposes only. No responsibility can be taken for any results or outcomes resulting from the use of this material. While every attempt has been made to provide information that is both accurate and effective, the author does not assume any responsibility for the accuracy or use/misuse of this information.

Yoga Poses Photos

Pixabay.com

Freepik.com

Dreamstime.com

Cover Design by Monique Joiner Siedlak

Cover Image by Pixabay.com

Logo Design by Monique Joiner Siedlak

Logo Image by Pixabay.com

Sign up to email list: www.mojosiedlak.com

Other Books in the Series

Yoga for Beginners

Yoga for Stress

Yoga for Back Pain

Yoga for Flexibility

Yoga for Advanced Beginners

Yoga for Fitness

Yoga for Runners

Yoga for Energy

Yoga for Your Sex Life

Yoga: To Beat Depression and Anxiety

Yoga for Menstruation

Table of Contents

Introduction

Yoga is not exactly the first exercise regimen you would think of when you first start your journey on to losing weight. You would think you would have to spend hours and hours in the gym lifting heavy weights, running till every drop of sweat is squeezed out of you and eat not a speck of food. Well, for some people that works. But as the old adage goes "Work smart, not hard" and that honestly is pretty applicable here with Yoga.

How Yoga Helps with Weight Loss

Yoga is surprisingly effective in helping you reduce that weight you have been meaning to put off for so long. To be honest, researchers are not exactly still sure why Yoga helps with reducing weight so much but theories point to how Yoga helps with regulating mental patterns. Yoga is known to bring actual happiness to those who practice it and this is because the poses and overall exercise help to bring changes in the mind.

These changes in the mental authority help reinforce positive changes in the system of the body and mind. All of this culminates with your body moving towards a healthier form. So both your mind and your body are being trained by your body.

The weight loss equation is a lot more complex that calories in, calories out – as the astounding results with Yoga prove. Research has shown that people tend to eat or rather over eat when they are faced with stress. This is to say, stress leads to an overall unhealthy diet. So it would not be crazy to assume that Yoga, a practice that is aimed to positively re-structure how your brain deals with stress and other related issues.

Warrior One Pose (Virabhadrasana)

The Warrior One Pose is the first of a series of three and is a focusing and strengthening pose, aimed to build a link, grounding you with the Earth's energy.

How to Do

Move your right foot toward the back of your mat to come into Warrior I. Bring your right heel to the floor and turn your right toes out to about a forty-five-degree angle. Bend your left knee over the left ankle. You might need to correct the length of your stance from the front to back. You can also broaden your stance from side to side for a greater stability. Maintain the position of your hips that same as it was in Mountain pose, with the hips pointing forward.

While breathing in, bring your arms up over your head. Your arm position may vary in relation to the flexibility in your shoulders. The typical position is with the palms touching above, but you may decide on keeping your palms apart at shoulder distance or you can bend at your elbows and open your arms resembling a saguaro cactus. A slight backbend will open the heart and the gaze move toward the fingertips.

Benefits

The Warrior One Pose helps strengthen and tone your arms, legs and lower back. It also helps increase stamina and improves the balance in your body.

Tip

Warrior One Pose has been shown with the heel of your front foot aligned with the arch of your back foot as if you were on a balance beam. This division enables the hips to square more.

Warrior Two Pose (Virabhadrasana II)

The Warrior Two Pose is the second of a sequence of three yoga poses that improve strength and stamina.

How to Do

From the Downward Facing Dog, step your left foot to the inside your left hand. Bend your left knee over your ankle so your thigh is parallel to the floor. Swivel on the ball of your right foot to bring your right heel to your mat. Your right foot should be at a 90-degree angle with the sole planted.

Your front heel is lined up with your back arch. Rise to stand. Open your hips to the right side of your mat. Your torso will face right. Extend your left arm toward the front of the mat and your right arm toward the back of the mat with your palms facing down. Keep both arms parallel to the floor. Release your shoulders away from your ears. Reach out through the fingertips of both hands.

Turn your head to face the front of your mat. Your gaze is forward over the left hand. Both thighs are rotating outward.

Engage your triceps to support your arms, your quadriceps to support your legs, and your belly to support your torso.

After several breaths, windmill your hands down to either side of your left foot and step back to Downward Dog. Stay here for a few breaths or go through a transition before repeating the pose with the right foot forward.

Benefits

Tones the abdomen, strengthen your legs and arms and opens your chest and shoulders.

Tip

When you bend the right knee to a right angle, bend it with a meaningful exhalation, and point the inside the right knee in the direction of the little-toe side of the right foot.

Warrior Three Pose (Virabhadrasana III)

The Warrior Three Pose is an intermediate balancing pose in yoga. This energetic standing posture builds stability throughout your whole body by incorporating all of the muscles through your core, arms, and legs.

How to Do

Begin in the Mountain Pose. With an exhale, move your right foot back about two feet, as you maintain your body weight forward on your left foot. Keep your left toes looking forward. Feel your left toes spread and find an even basis through the sole of your left foot. Put your hands on your hips to bring into line your hips and shoulders perpendicular to the front of your mat. Tighten your inner core muscles by pulling in the navel and waist.

Maintain a feeling you are holding the lower organs with a round band of muscle, then breathe in and raise your right foot as your incline your torso forward experiencing a hinging movement at your hips. Direct your stare straight down as you bend forward from your hips attaining a new focus.

As your torso and right leg go into a corresponding position with the floor, lengthen both legs without bracing into the bottom knee. The right hip may rise higher than the left. Keeping your right hip level with the left hip, experience a shift in a correct postural alignment. Imagine more length advancing into the right leg and spine. Maintain the digging into the left foot and tightening into the core muscles.

To intensify the influence of the balance, free your hands from your hips and elongate your arms straight out to the sides expanding your chest or forward in line with your head and neck. If you extend your arms forward, then turn your palms to face each other so your shoulder blades can draw down away from your ears. Breathe and stay here for five to ten breaths.

To release this pose, inhale as you lift your chest and place your right foot back into Mountain Pose. Exhale as you lower your arms, and draw a few breaths as you pause and then repeat on the right side for the same time.

Benefits

The Warrior III pose strengthens your legs, improves balance and your core strength.

Tip

You can either stand in front of the wall, bringing your arms outstretched in front of you with your hands on the wall or rotate and bring the raised back foot onto the wall. Both will give you the stability you require to level your hips. You can also hold on a chair as a substitute for using the wall.

Runner's Lunge Pose (Ardha Hanumanasana)

The Runner's Lunge yoga pose stretches your hamstrings they typically construct which for a good number of individuals. Tight hamstrings will influence your lower back. Maintaining your hamstrings flexibility will give you more freedom of movement.

How to Do

Begin in the Mountain Pose. Know the strength in your legs and the stability of your body. Breathe out and bend forward at your hip folds into a simple standing forward bend.

Stretch one leg back into a long lunge. Place your hands shoulder-width apart on either side of your front foot. Only the ball of your back foot is on the floor. It should extend your heel back. The knee of your front leg must be in alignment with your ankle. Release your groin muscles and sink the hips downwards to the floor.

Past the lengthening of the back heel, stretch the spine forward, outside the top of your head. Breathe in and open your upper body, looking forward somewhat.

To release this pose, you can either bring your front foot back in alignment with the back foot with your hands rooted or jump your back foot forward to meet the front foot into a standing forward bend. Walk your feet up to the hands into a basic forward bend. Breathe in and roll your spine back up into Mountain Pose. Repeat on another side.

Benefits

The Runner's Lunge pose stretches your groin and strengthening the legs and arms.

Tip

To maintain this pose longer, wedge a block in the middle of the floor and your back leg.

Inverted Triangle Pose (Parivritta Trikonasana)

The Inverted Triangle Pose is one of the more challenging poses for novices as well as advanced practitioners.

How to Do

Begin in the Mountain Pose. Step to the left with your left foot. Pivot your left foot ninety degrees and your right foot about fifteen degrees to the left. Bend your left leg ninety degrees. Extend your arms to your sides, with your palms up. Bend your torso to the left, with your left side facing your left thigh. Reach with your left arm down and right arm up.

Benefits

The Inverted Triangle pose strengthens your leg muscles. It helps sustain a proper balance of your body.

Tip

The Inverted Triangle pose is to some extent easier with a narrower stand. Beginners should likewise, place their hand to the inner foot, either on the floor or on a prop like a block or a chair.

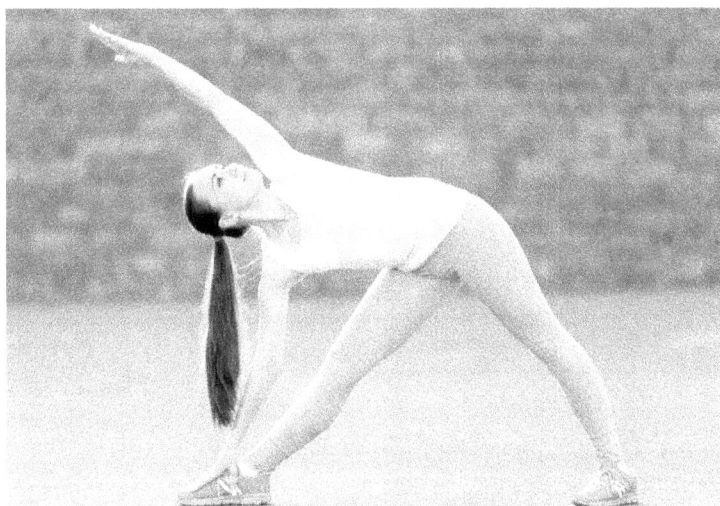

Chair Pose (Utkatasana)

The Chair Pose is a standing yoga posture that tones your entire body. The Chair Pose is an important component of Sun Salutations and is also often used as a transitional pose. It can also be practiced on its own to help build strength and stamina through your entire body.

How to Do

Begin with the Mountain Pose. Your big toes should be in contact of each other and your heels should be fixed a little apart. Your lower belly has to be drawn in a little to help support your spine. Move your shoulder blades downward keep your chest open and pushed out across your shoulders.

Take a deep breath and raise your arms over your head. You can keep your arms parallel to each other or just keep them up with the palms joined, facing inward. Your arms should be held at the same height or in front of your ears.

Bring your lower ribs toward your pelvis. At that point, breathe out and bend your knees. Try to make your thighs as parallel to the floor as you can. Your knees should come out in front of your feet. The torso should lean a little forward over the thighs till the torso makes a right angle with the upper part of the thighs. Your inner thighs should be parallel to each other and they should push the tops of your thigh bones to the heels.

Keep the edges of your shoulders firm. Bring your tailbone downward to the ground and towards your pubic bone to extend your lower back.

Remain in this pose for thirty seconds to one minute. To release, straighten your knees while you breathe in. Afterward, breathe out and bring your arms to the sides of your body, back into the Mountain Pose.

Benefits

The Chair pose exercises the spine, hips and chest muscles. It also helps to strengthen the lower back, torso and toning the thigh, ankle, leg and knee muscles.

Tip

Practice this near a wall to help you remain in the pose. You can stand with your back near the wall just a few inches away from it. Keep a proper distance to when you come into position, your tailbone comes into contact it then supported by the wall.

Plank Pose (Kumbhakasana)

As part of the Sun Salutation sequence, the Plank Pose is an arm balancing yoga pose that aids in tightening up your abdominal muscles and strengthening your arms and spine.

How to Do

This pose very similar to as if you were about to undertake a push-up. After completing the Downward Facing Dog, bring your hips forward till your shoulders are over your wrists and your entire body is in one straight line from the top of your head to your heels.

Be sure that your hips don't drop toward the floor or elevated up in the direction of the ceiling. Spreading out your fingers, push them down and balance on your palms. Bend your elbows and remember not to lock them.

Push back through your heels. Shift your shoulders away from your ears. Keeping your neck aligned with your spine, look towards the floor.

Benefits

The Plank Pose tones all the core muscles of the body, including the abdomen, chest, and low back. It strengthens the arms, wrists, and shoulders, and is often used to prepare the body for more challenging arm balances. Plank also strengthens the muscles surrounding the spine which improves posture.

Tip

When practicing the Plank Pose for several minutes, it will help builds endurance and stamina, while toning the nervous system.

Downward Facing Dog Pose (Adho Mukha Svanasana)

Downward Facing Dog Pose is one of the traditional Sun Salutation sequences poses. It's also an excellent yoga asana all on its own.

How to Do

Begin with your hands and knees in a tabletop position. Make sure your shoulders are aligned above your wrists and your hips are aligned above your knees. Come to a flat back by lengthening the spine. Place your head and neck in a non-aligned position, staring down in the direction of the floor.

Breathe out and raise your knees away from the floor. At the start, keep your knees slightly bent and your heels lifted away from the floor. Lengthen your tailbone positioned from the back of your pelvis and press it slightly toward the pubis. Alongside this tension, raise the resting bones in the direction of the ceiling, and from your inner ankles pull the inner legs up into the groin.

Followed by letting your breath out, push your top thighs back and extend your heels against or down toward the floor. Making sure that you do not lock them, straighten your knees and steady your outer thighs, rolling the upper thighs inward slightly, narrowing the front of the pelvis.

Firming the outer arms, press the bottoms of your index fingers assertively into the floor. From these two points, lift alongside the inside of your arms from the wrists to the tops of the shoulders. Firm your shoulder blades against your back then widen them and draw them toward the tailbone. Keep your head between your upper arms; not allowing it to simply hang.

Continue in this pose somewhere between one to three minutes. Afterward, bend your knees to the floor with a breath and repose in the Child's Pose.

Benefits

Downward Facing Dog pose can help decrease back pain through strengthening the whole back and shoulder girdle. It aids in stronger hands, wrists, the Achilles tendon, low-back, hamstrings, and calves, as well as increasing the full-body circulation. Elongates your shoulders and shoulder blade area. Decrease in tension and headaches by elongating the cervical spine and neck and relaxing the head. It can also lessen anxiety and expand your respiration

Tip

You can alleviate the burden on your wrists by employing a block beneath your palms or you can be capable of completing the pose upon your elbows. By lifting your hands on blocks or the seat of a chair, you can help to release and open your shoulders.

Dolphin Pose(Makarasana)

This intermediate pose will benefit those that are trying to get to headstands.

How to Do

From the Table Pose, lower your forearms to the floor folding the toes under and lift your hips upward to the ceiling. With the middle finger facing forward, spread the fingers wide apart, and your palms shoulder-width apart. Push the forearms, fingers and the palms into the floor, and push your hips up and back. Keeping the spine straight and long, reach up high by way of the tailbone.

Keep your feet at hip's width with the toes facing forward. Push the heels into the floor experiencing a stretch in the back of the legs. You can have a small bend at the knees to keep the back flat or your legs straight. Allow the head and neck fall freely from the shoulders; your forehead can rest on the floor.

Take breaths and hold for two to five breaths. To release this pose, come all the way down to Child's Pose or bend your knees and lower the hips back to the Table Pose.

Benefits

Dolphin is great for improving the upper body, with additional advantages include toning the arms, opening the shoulders, developing hip flexibility and strengthening the abdominals and back muscles.

Open your shoulders by lifting your elbows on a rolled-up sticky mat and pressing your inner wrists firmly to the floor.

Tip

Novices can raise their elbows while doing the Dolphin Pose along with keeping their wrists pushed into the floor. This can help in opening up the shoulders minus any extra stress. To reduce strain on the neck region you can support the head with the use of a pillow or folded blanket.

Four-Limbed Staff Pose (Chaturanga Dandasana)

The Four-Limbed Staff Pose is also frequently known as the half-push up. When done correctly, your body resembles a staff or rod, with the spine in one straight line. It is a fundamental component of the Sun Salutations.

How to Do

Bringing your hands shoulder-width apart; supporting your shoulders, elbows, and wrists. Bend your arms straight back, keeping the upper arms hugging into your sides as you lower down toward the floor.

Engage your core and keep your hips raised up creating a line of energy from the crown of your head through your heels. Stop when your forearms and upper arms are at a right angle. So your shoulders are at the same level with your elbows. Hold the pose for ten to thirty seconds, taking four deep breaths. Release with an exhalation.

Benefits

The Four-Limbed Staff Pose tones and strengthens your abs. Builds muscle upper arms, back, and shoulders and wrists.

Tip

For beginners, bring your knees to the floor until you can build enough strength to hold your body up with the arms.

Keep in mind that your neck remains balanced. Your eyes are to the floor. Allowing your body to lower below your elbows can cause elbow strain. If you have wrist conditions, for instance, carpal tunnel syndrome, you should avoid this pose.

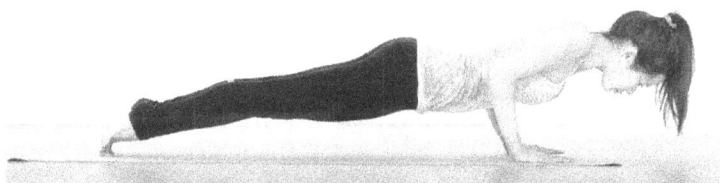

Upward-Facing Dog Pose (Urdhva Mukha Svanasana)

Upward Facing Dog Pose is one of the most generally recognized, as easily as Downward Dog Pose, and recognized yoga pose due to its many benefits and healing purposes. Similar to the Cobra Pose, it is thought of as one of the simplest of the back-bending poses and is regularly carried out during the traditional Sun Salutation sequence.

How to Do

Lie face down on the floor. Extend your legs back, keeping the tops of your feet on the floor. As you bend your elbows, stretch your palms on the floor at the side of your waist, as a result, your forearms are somewhat erect to the floor.

Breathe in and push your inner hands steadily into the floor and slightly back, comparable to trying to force yourself in a forward motion along the floor. Then at the same time, straighten your arms and lift your torso up and your legs a few inches off the floor on an intake breath. Keep the thighs firm and somewhat turned in, the arms steady and turned out to the elbow creases facing forward.

Push your tailbone in the direction of your pubis and lift pubis toward your navel. Contract the hip positions. Stiffen but do not totally harden the buttocks.

Steady your shoulder blades adjacent to the back and puff the side ribs forward. Raise through the upper part of the sternum, however, make an effort not to push the front ribs forward. It will prompt the lower back to tighten. You will at that point look forward or you can angle your head towards the back slightly, remembering to take care not to constrict the back of your neck and the tightening of your throat.

Even though Upward Facing Dog Pose is one of the poses utilized in the classic Sun Salutation Sequence, you can correspondingly practice this pose independently, maintaining the pose fifteen to thirty seconds, inhaling slowly. Release back to the floor or rise into the Downward Facing Dog Pose along with an exhalation.

Benefits

The Upward Facing Dog assists in opening the chest and strengthens the whole body and aligns the spine and invigorates nervous system and the kidneys.

Tip

Performing Upward Facing Dog will elongate and strengthen your whole body. You can utilize it as a backbend by itself, or as a transition for even deeper backbends.

Cobra Pose (Bhujangasana)

The Cobra Pose is a familiar Yoga backbend. When you perform the Cobra Pose, you stretch the front of your torso and spine.

How to Do

Lie face down on the floor. Extend your legs back, with the tops of your feet on the floor. Stretch your hands on the floor beneath your shoulders. Squeeze the elbows back into your body. Push the tops of your feet, thighs, and pubis powerfully into the floor.

On an inhalation, start to straighten your arms to raise your chest off the floor. Go only to a height at which you can sustain a connection throughout your pubis to your legs. Press your tailbone toward the pubis and raise the pubis toward your navel. Narrow the hip, compressing but don't harden your buttocks.

Firm the shoulder blades against the back, puffing the side ribs forward. Lift through the top of the sternum but avoid pushing the front ribs forward, which only hardens the lower back. Distribute the backbend evenly throughout the full spine.

Hold the pose anywhere from fifteen to thirty seconds, breathing freely. Release back to the floor with an exhalation.

Benefits

The Cobra Pose is best known for its capability to build up the flexibility of your spine. It stretches the chest along with strengthening your spine and shoulders. It further assists in opening the lungs and stimulating the abdominal organs, improving digestion.

An energizing backbend, the Cobra Pose can reduce stress and fatigue. It also firms and tones the shoulders, abdomen, and buttocks, and assists in easing back pain.

Tip

The Cobra Pose will be able to energize and warm up the body, getting it ready for the deeper backbends in your yoga routine.

Half Lord of Fishes Pose (Ardha Matsyendrasana)

The Half Lord of Fishes Pose is a moderate to intense twist that encourages length of your spine, a base stretch for your outer hips, and brings forth growth through the chest and shoulders.

How to Do

Begin in a seated position with your legs straight in front of you. Bring in your knees up and bend them with the purpose of your feet are now flat on the floor. This is your beginning position. Bring your right leg beneath your left leg. Maintain your left leg in the starting position. Your right leg should bend at the knee and then keep close to your hip.

Taking your left leg, cross it over the left knee. Set your left foot flat on the floor on the outside of your right knee. Bring your right arm and reach up. Next slowly bend your arm at the elbow and place your elbow on your left knee. Take your left arm and place behind your back and use for a base.

Breathe in and out while either turning your head opposite to the way your back is stretching, or you can turn your head with your back.

Benefits

The Half Lord of Fishes Pose can restore and improve spinal range of motion. It also beneficial for backaches.

Tip

Maintain your right leg extended if you cannot steadily tuck it beneath your left buttock. Squeeze the left knee with your right arm if that feels better than bringing the right elbow outside the left knee. If you normally use a blanket or other prop under your sit bones for seated poses, it's fine to do that here as well.

Boat Pose (Navasana)

The Boat Pose is a great challenging yoga pose, but also a beneficial one. It builds core strength, stability, and awareness of posture, strengthening the abdominal and hip muscles.

How to Do

Start in a seated posture with your knees bent and your feet flat on the floor. Raise your feet off the floor. Maintain your knees bent at the beginning. Bring your shins parallel to the floor. This is the Half Boat Pose.

Your torso will want to instinctively fall back, but do not let your spine round.

If you can do so without losing the form of your upper body, straighten out your legs to a forty-five-degree angle. You want to hold your torso as vertical as possible so it creates a V shape with the legs.

Roll your shoulders backward and straighten your arms approximately parallel to the floor with your palms spun up. Balance on the sitting bones. Stay for at least five breaths.

Benefits

Builds strength and steadiness at the body's core and intensely challenges the abdomen, spine, and hip flexors.

Tip

You can, if it helps you to hold your spine straight, hold the backs of your thighs with your hands.

Butterfly Pose (Baddha Konasana)

The Butterfly Pose is a seated pose that strengthens and opens your hips and groin while decreasing abdominal pain.

How to Do

Sit with your knees near to your chest. Relax your knees out to each side and slightly press the bottoms of your feet together. Hold on to your ankles or feet.

Benefits

The Butterfly Pose is a good stretch for your inner thighs, groins, and knees. It helps improve the flexibility in your groin and hip area. When standing and walking for long hours, it removes fatigue.

Can give assistance from menstrual discomfort and menopause symptoms and smooth delivery if it's practiced on a regular basis until late pregnancy. Also helps in intestine and bowel movement.

Tip

You may find it difficult to lower your knees toward the floor. If your knees are incredibly high and your back is rounded, be sure to sit on a high support, even as high as a foot off the floor.

Locust Pose (Salabhasana)

The Locust Pose is a transitional backbend that strengthens and tones the whole back of your body.

How to Do

Lying prone (on your stomach), push your chin against the mat. Keeping your hands in fists with thumbs inside, put your straight arms beneath your thighs. Extend your legs straight behind you, hip-width apart. Make an effort with your back muscles and supporting with your fists from below, use your inner thighs to lift your legs up toward the ceiling, raising both your legs up. Keep this position without holding your breath.

Benefits

The Locust Pose opens your shoulders and neck while it strengthens the back and abdomen. It also eases upper-back aches.

Tip

Roll a blanket and position it at the bottom of your rib cage if you're not gaining much lift in your chest. Practicing like this way will help you strengthen your back muscles.

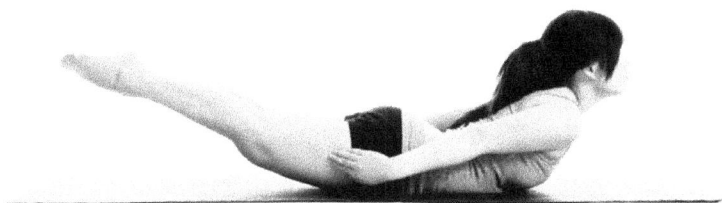

Fish Pose (Matsyasana)

The Fish Pose is performed often as a counterbalance poses to the Shoulder Stand Pose. It stretches your upper body in the opposite way. The Fish Pose has a lot of possibilities because it encourages the throat and crown.

How to Do

Begin by lying on your back. Keeping your feet are together, relax your hands at the side of the body. Inhale. With palms facing down, place the hands underneath your hips. Draw your elbows close to each other and exhale.

Elevate your head and chest, and then inhale. You should extend your legs with your head relaxed back, without adding pressure on your head.

Keeping the chest elevated, lower the head backward and touch the top of your head to the floor. Exhale; allow the chest to open finding awareness of relaxed backbend.

Hold this pose for as long as you can while taking soothing long breaths in and out. With each exhalation, relax in the pose. Raise your head, while lowering your chest and head to the floor. Bring your hands back along the sides of your body and relax.

Benefits

The Fish Pose can help headaches caused by stiffness of the neck. It relaxes Spinal Cord and back muscle tissues. It aids in relieving asthma and respiratory disorders. This yoga pose, when practiced regularly, helps to remedy impotence. Also eases anxiety, mild backache, fatigue and menstrual pain.

Tip

If your head does not comfortably come to the floor, position a blanket or block under your head or slightly lower your chest.

Garland Pose (Malasana)

The Garland Pose is a hip-opening yoga posture that aids in lengthening and opening the hips. An excellent pose to ground yourself.

How to Do

Begin by squatting with your feet as close together as possible, keeping your heels on the floor if you can; otherwise, support them on a folded mat.)

Separate your thighs somewhat wider than your torso. While exhaling, lean your torso forward and fit it between your thighs.

Pressing your elbows against your inner knees, move your palms to together in the Salutation Seal, by pressing your palms and fingers and together. To expand, push your inner thighs against the edges of your torso. Bring your arms forward. Next swing them out to the sides and spot your shins into your armpits. Pressing your fingertips to the floor, or reaching around the outside of your ankles, hold onto your back heels.

Hold this position for thirty seconds to one minute. Next, inhale, straighten your knees, and stand back into the Standing Half Forward.

Benefits

The Garland Pose works at stretching your ankles, groins and back torso and tones the belly

Tip

If you find squatting is difficult, try sitting on the front edge of a chair, with your thighs forming a right angle to your torso. Keep your heels on the floor ahead of your knees. And lean your torso forward between the thighs.

Constructing a Yoga Sequence

Here are a few points to keep in mind how to construct a yoga sequence. You are not at a studio, paying to be there. You do not have to exercise for over an hour. Begin with 5-10 minutes. Notice how you feel by the end of this time. If you feel as if you can do more, go ahead. If no, end your routine there.

Start with 5-10 minutes. By the conclusion of that time, notice how you feel. Do you desire to resume? If yes, continue for an extra five minutes and then check in with yourself once more. If not, close your workout.

The same as any physical journey, a yoga sequence has three clear parts.

Your opening or warm-up sequence

You don't want to jump into the main event tight and cold. This is where you move through and loosening up your major muscle groups as well as body parts

Your main sequence

Once you've warmed up, it's time for your main sequence. This component of your sequence is influenced by the goal of your routine. If it's an asymmetrical pose, keep in mind to do both sides and devote about the same time on each side.

The closing or cool down sequence

Now you've completed the principal portion of your yoga practice, it's time to cool down.

About The Author

Monique Joiner Siedlak is a writer, witch, and warrior on a mission to awaken people to their greatest potential through the power of storytelling infused with mysticism, modern paganism, and new age spirituality. At the young age of 12, she began rigorously studying the fascinating philosophy of Wicca. By the time she was 20, she was self-initiated into the craft, and hasn't looked back ever since. To this day, she has authored over 35 books pertaining to the magick and mysteries of life. Her most recent publication is book one of an Urban Paranormal series entitled "Jaeger Chronicles."

Originally from Long Island, New York, Monique is now a proud inhabitant of Northeast Florida; however, she considers herself to be a citizen of Mother Earth. When she doesn't have a book or pen in hand, she loves exploring new places and learning new things. And being the nature lover that she is, she considers herself to be an avid animal advocate.

To find out more about Monique Joiner Siedlak artistically, spiritually, and personally, feel free to visit her **official website**.

Other Books by Monique Joiner Siedlak

Mojo's Wiccan Series

Wiccan Basics

Candle Magick

Wiccan Spells

Love Spells

Abundance Spells

Hoodoo

Herb Magick

Seven African Powers: The Orishas

Moon Magick

Cooking for the Orishas

Creating Your Own Spells

Body Mind and Soul Series

Creative Visualization

Astral Projection for Beginners

Meditation for Beginners

Reiki for Beginners

Thorne Witch Series

The Phoenix

Beautiful You Series

Creating Your Own Body Butter

Creating Your Own Body Scrub

Creating Your Own Body Spray

Mojo's Self-Improvement Series

Manifesting With the Law of Attraction

Stress Management

Jaeger Chronicles

Glen Cove

Connect With Me!

I really appreciate you reading my book! Please leave a review and let me know your thoughts. Here are the social media locations you can find me at:

Like my Facebook Page: www.facebook.com/mojosiedlak

Follow me on Twitter: www.twitter.com/mojosiedlak

Follow me on Instagram: www.instagram.com/mojosiedlak

Follow me on Bookbub: http://bit.ly/2KEMkqt

Sign up to my Email List at www.mojosiedlak.com and receive a free book!

If you enjoyed this book or found it useful I'd be very grateful if you'd post a short review at your retailer. Your support really does make a difference and I read all the reviews personally so I can get your feedback and make this as well as the next book even better.